T0103594

Mistaken for Love

FIRST ADDITION

KEYTA HOUSE

WESTBOW®
PRESS
A DIVISION OF THOMAS NELSON
& ZONDERVAN

Reference to Bible:
Zondervan KJV Study Bible, Barker, Kenneth, 1985.

Reference: Webster on line source
Webster.com

WestBow Press books may be ordered through
booksellers or by contacting:

WestBow Press
A Division of Thomas Nelson & Zondervan
1663 Liberty Drive
Bloomington, IN 47403
www.westbowpress.com
1 (866) 928-1240

ISBN: 978-1-4908-3977-6 (sc)
ISBN: 978-1-4908-3978-3 (e)

Library of Congress Control Number: 2014910262

Printed in the United States of America.

WestBow Press rev. date: 2/5/2015

Contents

Discover the authentic meaning of Love in this profound workbook entitled "Mistaken for Love" written by Keyta House. Embark on an adventure that will impact, revive and heal the substance of the heart.

Thank You!

Thank You God! I give all praises to my Almighty God that is the giver of life and salvation! Thank you God for all that you are to me! I celebrate You God alone for your greatness! I soak in your "True" unfailing unconditional Love! I live in your grace, mercy and blessings that you pour into and on me every day. I worship you God with my life. Thank you God for giving me this awesome revelation about your precious Love to share with your people. Thank you God for speaking into my life and to my family and healing our hearts. I dedicate this book to my God.

Forever grateful,
Your daughter Keyta House

Thank you!

There are so many people that I extend my appreciation too. I cannot say Thank you enough to all of my family, friends, and to the people of God. Thank you! Thank you! Thank you! Thank you to my Mother Barbara James (T.James-Step Dad). Thank you for always believing in me and loving me. You are the Queen in my life. Thank you to Mama & Papa. I love you both more than you could ever know. Thank you to my sister, Tina Spell (Roy Spell: Brother-in-Law) my biggest fan. You always cheer for me! Thank you to my baby sister Ramona House. I love you! Thank you to my Editor Kamesa. Special Shout out to my three amazing brothers Keith, Adrian, and Marcus James! You guys are the best! Thank you to both my family and extended family. You all have made a great impact on my life. Thank you Apostle and Prophetess Kittrell for imparting "worship" into my life. Thank you to my Pastor,

Pastor C. Albritton of Your Day of Deliverance for pushing me and teaching me. I love you so very much Pastor. Thank you to my adopted Mother, Auradis C. Griffin (Mr. Ambrose). You encourage me. Thank you for every "Bless Your Heart!" Thank you to my adopted Dad, Walter L. Worsley Senior. Thank you to all the Men and Women of God that have, taught, trained, and spoken into my life. You have all been a tremendous blessing in my life. Thank you to all of my "friends." Thank you for your support. Thank you to my three handsome boys, Keyontae, Cha'ron, and Caleb Worsley. You have always been there for Mommy. You each hold a very dear place in my heart! Mommy loves you all so very much! Last but certainly not least, thank you to my very best friend, Gregory Bosworth. I could never tell you Thank you enough for your continued support, your encouragement, and for all that you do. You truly are a blessing in my life. I love you dearly.

No Greater Love

There is no greater Love than that shown by God, allowing His only begotten Son to be hung upon a rugged cross until death to rise again for the benefit and salvation of the people whom He created and passionately loved. However, in today's society, love is being mistaken and misrepresented by the images of sex, kind gestures; self-geared attractions, poor modeled relationships and in countless other ways. For example, some mistakenly consider Love to be a mixture of kind words combined with the emotion of appreciation. Others identify love with a touch which is generated from the flesh. Then there are those that associate love with attraction. This love is based off the definition of the human eye, considering details such as the shade of one's skin, formation of muscles, or length of a person's hair. All of these distinctive differences are combined together producing the calculating factors of love based merely off observation. As young adults we accumulate our own individual perception of love mirrored into our hearts and minds by our interactions with our family, friends, society, the church, and other sources. Our interpretation of Love is based off what we are given. In some cases that was the soft touch of your Mother's hand on your cheek to wipe away a tear. For others, that was Daddy coming home drunk and beating Mother to a faint pulse. Love, has historically been misrepresented from generation to generation and has completely obtained a disfigured face.

Defining Love

Webster defines love as emotion of a strong affection and personal attachment. Love is also a virtue representing all of human kindness, compassion, and affection—"the unselfish loyal and benevolent concern for the good of another." Love may describe actions towards others or oneself based on compassion or affection (Webster.com).

In **English, love refers to** a variety of different feelings, states, and attitudes, ranging from pleasure to interpersonal attraction. Love may refer specifically to the passionate desire and intimacy of **romantic love**, to **sexual love** of Eros (intimate love), to the emotional closeness of **familial love**, to the **platonic love** (a love that is non-sexual) that defines friendship, or the profound oneness or devotion of and meanings, combined with the complexity of the feelings involved, makes love unusually difficult to consistently define, compared to other emotional states. (Webster.com)

Simply put, love is established into the heart of men and women today for various reasons. Fortunately, **the Bible** gives us an un-complex **definition for Love** in **I John 4: 8 "He that loveth not, knoweth not God; for God is Love."**

Where did we go wrong?

So, where did we go wrong? Why has love been misrepresented for so long? Why are young men showing love through violence? Why are young ladies obsessed with youthful pregnancies outside of marriage? Why are relationships openly accepted without commitment? Why is the rate of divorce rising in our communities? Why do we openly disrespect our leaders, our Pastors, our husbands, our wives, our children, and even ourselves? Why do we allow ourselves to create social cliques in the church? Why do we open the door for the spirit of division to enter our churches? Why do we subconsciously say that we don't judge by the status of our bank accounts or by the brands of our clothing but consciously segregate the people in our minds? Some even operate as judge and jury of others forgetting that they too were once sinners before Jesus graciously saved their precious souls. When and where did we decide as a culture, as a society to become comfortable as a culture, as a society to become comfortable with disrespecting each other?

The Single Mom

Why are we gossiping about the **young girl with the three children** by three different men? Why doesn't one of the Mothers of the church embrace her with the unconditional love that Jesus Christ our Lord and Savior has shown toward us? Instead, we openly judge and criticize, chasing her away from the true hope that God intended for her to have in His house. She is rejected once again. Not only have multiple partners disregarded her, as well as her family who has broken her down through the years with words of disappointment, but now she faces the same rejection in the one place that was intended to be her sanctuary: the church. All she wanted was a hug. All her three children needed was for Mommy to be healed. They are all broken, shattered into pieces. The structure of the family completely unbalanced. She is overwhelmed by the pressures of life and the poor choices she made in her own will. She struggles alone to find a way out. She needs God. She knows there is something so much bigger than her. She just needed a hug; a touch of trust, sincerity, love and compassion from you. She walks out of the front doors of the church, dragging the youngest child, and yelling at the other two as the warm tears run down her cheek and the pain of aching heart penetrates into the very depths of her soul. She intimately says to herself "**All I want is love**."

The Newly Weds

Next, we have the **Newly-Wed couple**. They have just gotten married. The honey moon stage is surely fading away as they face the challenges of everyday life. The enemy is attacking them left and right. She is frustrated and her husband doesn't know what to do. They long for the wisdom of the seasoned couples in their church home; however, the sisters are too busy looking at him instead of praying with her. The deacons have no time to support their brother in the Lord because they have more important matters to attend to such as meetings regarding the next Deacon Appreciation service. Three years later they are divorced and both married to new partners with unhealed hearts and in complete deception of what "true" love really is. An endless cycle of mistakes repeated over and over again continue into their new marriages and unhealthy habits are passed on to their children. No one told them where the source of love came from during their marriage.

The Young Man

Now, we see the **Young Man** in his name brand polo shirt and sagging designer jeans. He has a couple of kids around town with two different "Baby Mamas." He is popular amongst the youth. All they see are his fancy twenty inch rims when he passes by. All that can be heard is the bass in his speaker box in the trunk of his refurbished 1960 freshly painted Buick. When we pass him, we lock our doors. We don't even smile. We look straight ahead as the assumptive fear about the young man penetrates the thoughts in our minds. Why do we disrespect this young man with our ignorance? The frown upon his face stems from the thought of the little boy inside wanting the father he never had. How can he be a father to his children when he himself doesn't even know what a father is. How can he stand tall in confidence, when the world tells him he is a dead beat dad, a thief, and bound for prison? How can he transfer the success of his life onto his children when all he has heard since he was born is that he is a failure and will be nothing more than his father? How can he believe in anything else, when the world gives him absolutely no hope? He needs a chance to hear and feel who God created him to be. He needs the unconditional Love of His almighty Father, God.

Where has the passion gone in the church?

Too good to Love

Did we become too sanctified, too holy, and **too good to love**? Where has the passion in the church gone? We were on fire as young babes in the Lord! You couldn't get us to stop professing the unfailing Love of our Great God. We outwardly expressed the depths of our gratitude for our Savior Jesus Christ to every person we encountered. But, somehow for some of us, the more mature we thought we had become in Christ, the less we were able to express this passionate Love. Instead, we judged, pointed fingers, got into our groups, and simply put, began to live by the mentality of "Let the best man prosper." What happened to sacrifice? What happened to humility? What happened to submission? What happened to loving thy neighbor as thyself as the Bible instructs us to in Matthew 19:19? We made an open confession to God for forgiveness of our sins and made an invitation for Jesus to be in our lives as our personal Savior. We embraced the unconditional love of our God. We clinched the love that fell into our lives to make us whole and brand new. This great Love that we opened our hearts to washed us in the precious blood of Jesus Christ and removed all of our blemishes. Did we forget what God did for us? Did we forget how we used to be? Did we forget how bad of a situation we were in when God patiently waited on us to turn to Him? Why do we now so easily reject each other in the church? Why is love so difficult to share in our churches today? Somewhere we have managed to lose love.

Something Happened

Somewhere we know that something happened. How did the passion of love escape from the hearts of the people of God? What could be strong enough to pull God's people away from the principles of Love He imparted into us? The Bible tells us in

Romans Chapter 8:38-39
"For I am persuaded, that neither death, nor life, nor angels, nor principalities, nor powers, nor things present, nor things to come, nor height, nor depth, nor any other creature, shall be able to separate us from the love of God, which is in Christ Jesus our Lord."

How did we get disconnected? Let's explore together how this happened. One day one word became an action. One action became a habit. One habit became a way of life. A way of life became a "tradition" amongst the people of God. This is how we got to where we are in some of our churches today. Not only did we disrespect ourselves, but we allowed Satan to use us to disrespect our God. By not allowing Him to move by His almighty power and we constricted Him to the wills of our "tradition."

Activity I

Activity I Part I

Part I: Let's go back to the world's definition of Love. Let's look at some of the words the world uses in every day conversation, in songs, and their actions to express love.

Hate | Steal | Cheat | Misdirect | No belief |

Profanity | Lie | Mislead | Un-passionate |

Ugly | Manipulate | Silence | Unresponsive

| Unconcerned | Stupid | Thoughtless |

Made to feel Guilty | Unproductive | Unsuccessful

| Idiot | Unworthy | Worthless | No expectations |

Activity I Part I continued

Unreliable | Better | No Value | Not good enough |

Without purpose | Unidentified | No place to fit in

| Lonely | No Goals | Death | No life | Threatened |

Without reason | Old | Used | Abused | Battered

| Unsafe | Unprotected | Unsure | Unsettled

| Disrespected | Obscene Profanity | Cocky |

Cry Baby | Useless | Too Sensitive | Immature

| Selfish | A nobody | Self-Righteousness

| Dead | Wishing Death | Forgotten

Activity I

Activity I Part II:

Let's have a brief discussion about the words in Activity I, Part I.

- Where did these words come from?
- How do these words make you feel?
- Who has said these words to you?
- In what types of places did you hear these words? For example, home, church, etc.
- How do you react when you hear these words?
- How do you communicate back with the person who uses these words with you?
- Do you use these words when you talk to other people?
- Do these words bother you or are they okay in day to day conversation in your life?

Take a brief evaluation of the words you use.
Do you need to remove some words and replace
them with others?

Write your thoughts below for personal
reflections:

_____

_____

_____

_____

_____

_____

_____

_____

_____

_____

_____

_____

_____

It's All a Mistake!

We often mistake the words in **Activity I** for love. Unfortunately, in some cases they have become the only form of emotions that we can identify with due to **the lack of the true source of Love which is God**. The Bible tells us in I John 4:9; **"He that loveth not, knoweth not God; for God is love."** How can we identify with something that we know nothing about? How can we then give what isn't a part of us away to others? How can we love our children, our spouses, most importantly ourselves? Where do we begin to nurture our minds, our souls, and our hearts? At this point, we walk around aimlessly throwing around the very opposite of Love: hate, abuse, and discontentment just to name a few. No wonder there is a very common saying of "Hurt people, hurt people." People of God, how can we change? How can we end the hurt in the church? How can we restore our families, marriages, and again most importantly ourselves? We must go back to the original source. We must **find our way back to Love; God.**

Let's find the starting line and begin our journey back to Love, back to our Awesome creator: God. Perhaps you already knew about Love and had a relationship with God but have now found yourself distant with God. Maybe someone or something came between you and God: your career, repetitive encounters in bad relationships with friends, women, men, family, etc., negligent choices, bad decisions, mistakes you thought you had made that could never be forgiven. *(Condemnation of your- self)* Now is the time to restore the greatest love back into your life. God loves you and He never ever stopped loving you.

Experiences of Life

"The Great Wall of China"

Throughout different life experiences and relation-ships, we find ourselves afraid to love after encoun-tering various sources of discomfort. The feeling we get after being lied to, cheated on, disappointed, rejected, insulted, and even tormented often times leads us to building the **"Great Wall of China"** around our hearts. No one comes in, and no one goes out. This creates a feeling of numbness; am-bivalence to emotions. What if Jesus had done that in turn to us for what the people did to Him? What if He rejected you and me, a people he had never seen before, because of the relationships he encoun-tered with the people who beat Him, mocked Him, tormented Him, lied to Him and hurt Him? What a profound question. What if He gave up His love for us like you did? What if He closed His heart and decided to never trust again? He didn't give up on

Love, thanks be unto God! So whether it be a failed marriage that has left you broken hearted, a bad experience in the church or that man or woman that left you standing alone at the altar; maybe a parent or family member that has rejected you; or perhaps you've seen your spouse with another woman or man in your bed. No matter what you must forgive. Yes, even if you who were raped and deprived of your very innocence, molested by your father, step father, uncle, brother, any other family member, or by a complete stranger. If you are murdered by hate itself inside your soul, *You* must first forgive and Trust God to love; for with-out Love you don't have God. Your very life depends on it. **You must love again!**

You have a Choice

Every imaginable hurt beneath the sun can be healed by God if that is truly what you desire.

You have a choice. You can choose to stay in the condition that you are in currently; you can remain bitter, broken, disconnected and conform to hate. Or you can choose to allow God to heal you and love again and you can chose to grow and have peace beyond all understanding. What will you choose for your life today? The choice is yours.

It doesn't matter what you did or what that person, thing or situation did to you. There is nothing too big for God. Again I ask you, what will your choice be? It's all in your hands.

You have control. What do you want for your life? What are you worth? What do you deserve? It's all about you at this very moment. There is no one else here but you and your God. What will you say to Him?

You Can Be Healed!

It is my prayer that you will begin the healing process today. You don't have to linger a second longer in the pain and hurt you have felt for years. You can change your position in life. Your pain was meant to birth out the greatness in you. Yes, even your pain has a purpose in your life! It was not sent to kill, steal and destroy, as the enemy made it to appear; but to increase your strength and the power of God inside of you. Yes, your pain came to bring forth undefeatable life inside of you! It wasn't designed to have you stagnated in depression, contemplating suicide, or absent from Love. You can endure every tragic experience in your life with the gracious perfected Love of God! You can begin the process first by forgiving yourself and acknowledging the truth that you are now embracing. Don't allow people, circumstances or anything else to hold you captive a second longer. Forgive every person that has every hurt you. You know what Love is and now you can forgive. Let God heal you and make you whole.

With Out Love

Let's talk about life without love. What happens when you don't have the presence of Love in your life. Life without it is full of fear, emptiness, and sadness. There is no passion in or for living without love in a person's life. There is no concern for anything. Life becomes aimless, with no direction. The desires of a person without love is driven from a place of selfishness which stems from the rotten roots of a broken heart. These people in turn break the hearts of those that surround them. People are hopeless and sometime are lead to successful suicidal attempts leading to death when Love is absent from the heart, mind, body, and soul.

With Out Love....

The bible informs us in the book of **Corinthians**, chapter 13 beginning at the fourth verse thru verse eight what happens when we operate outside of love. Let's take a look at what the word of God tells us when we take love out of the equation.

I Corinthians 13:1 **"Though I speak with the tongues of men and of angels, and have not charity, I am become as sounding brass or tinkling cymbal"**

Though a person speak with the beauty of authentic language of mankind and the harmonic sound of angels, when spoken without charity (LOVE) it creates the reckless sound of crashing brass and cymbals dropped upon a cement floor

*noise-a loud disagreeable sound

When we speak without Love, it is just noise. For example, when you say "Good Morning" in a monotone voice with no Love, it is as offensive as noise to the person to which you spoke. That person can recognize that your "Good Morning" was not genuine. The atmosphere can be changed by what you speak. The word tells us in.

Proverbs 18:21 "Death and life *are* in the power of the tongue, And those who love it will eat its fruit." This is how the words in Activity I on page 16 and 17 became alive. We began to communicate with each other outside the parameters of Love. Instead we engaged with each other with the very opposite of Love: HATE. The attributes of hate (the absence of love) began to grow amongst God's people. Little by little, we as a body accepted the absence of Love (God).

With Out Love....

<u>I Corinthians 13:2</u>

"And though I have a gift of prophecy and understand all mysteries, all knowledge; and though I have all faith; so that I could remove mountains, and have no charity, I am nothing."

Although I (you) have a Great gift of prophecy understanding mysteries, all knowledge and have faith that can move a mountain without charity (LOVE), I (you) are nothing.

*The word **<u>nothing</u>** is defined as: not anything, a person or thing considered of little or no importance (2) a thing that does not exist (3) zero; in vain, without reason, free (standing with of for No CAUSE). Your value becomes equal to zero when you operate outside of Love.*

How can we as the people of a Living GOD prophesy without charity (Love)? How can we share revelation and knowledge without charity (Love)? How can we prophesy without charity if charity is Love and Love is God? How can we prophesy without God? God gives the vision; God speaks the truth and we are only able to speak into our established future through and by God. How can we believe without God? God puts His good self on our mind to give us the desire and passion to believe.

When people prophesy over the people of God without God and without His compassion, it can lead to the sowing of unbelief in the people who are receiving the prophecy. Those individuals may also reject what God is saying to them because of your composure.

__With Out Love....__

Continued....

Unbelief creates nonproductive faith which is dead and this profits the body of Christ absolutely nothing. So, all that prophesying that has been done in the absence of Love (GOD) was done in vain. Understanding mysteries without Love keeps the body of Christ confined. You have to have charity (Love which is God) in order to obtain understanding and even if you do have faith, without the presence of charity (Love which is God) you allow the feeling of doubt to come in. The people of God will not feel you are trustworthy and will in turn reject the word that God is instructing you to give to them. Lack of faith in what you bring forth and ultimately death in the body of Christ. In perfect Love there is no fear. You allow fear to come in, torment the minds of God's people when you are not obedient to God's word and operate outside of His love.

With Out Love....

I Corinthians 13:3: "And though I bestow all my goods to feed the poor, and though I give my body to be burned, and have no charity; it profit me nothing."

You can give all that you have away, sacrifice even your body to be burned, but without charity (Love: affection, love for one's fellow human); it profit (You) nothing. All of your efforts and sacrifice was done in vain.

What is the word telling us? You can give all that you have. You can donate to the local charity every year. You can begrudgingly give to the church all you have to support the building fund every time it's due and give all the money and material good that you have away. You could even allow your body to burned; the very flesh of you. Think about it. The thought of man sacrificing his very body, being overwhelmed with the gashing pain of burning fire upon his flesh. Guess what? All of these things amount to nothing. They have no value at all without the presence of Love. Without God in the equation you have done nothing in the site of Him or your brother. How many times have we done any of these things? How many times have we given for our own selfish reasons? How many times have you given in order to look good to other people or even offered a hand because you don't want to be told you have to? How many times have you sacrificed without the Love of God in your heart? This is between you and God. Answer inwardly, correct any wrong and repent now. Do not repent just because you feel bad, but allow a radical change that will transfer healing and permanent deliverance in your life! Don't allow the greatness in you to be wasted. Your greatness, your sacrifice, your giving, it is done with power. You have the authority over your giving. Your offerings and your tithes are obedient to you and can be sent out with an assignment but only if given with Love. This principle also applies when you give of yourself. Make sure that you are giving in love before you give anything. If not, you have done it all in vain.

The Characteristics of Love

Now, our journey takes a transition into a new direction. We have discussed how we got to the point of operating without love. We found that allowing each other to disrespect one another has lead to where some of us are today: a lonely road without any sign of hope. We learned what happens when we give without love and how our lives are affected when we don't have it personally. It's time to take a drastic turn in the right direction. Let's discover the characteristics of Love. What does real love feel like? What does love act like? What are the characteristics of Love? How should we feel if we have love? There are so many questions about Love. God has the answer for them all. The book of Corinthians teaches us about the absence of love and it also teaches us about the characteristics of love. Let's see what else God has to say to us about love. Here we grow together in love.

The Characteristics of Love

I Corinthians 13: 4-8

I Corinthians 13:4

"Charity suffereth long, and is kind; charity envieth not; charity vaunteth not itself, is not puffed up."

Charity (Love) suffereth (the bearing of pain distress) long (measuring in space or time, of greater or unusual length, quantity etc., far reaching, well supplied, from start to finish) is (to be) kind (sympathetic, benevolent (benevolence: well-wishing and indignation to do good kindliness); charity (love) envieth (discontent and ill will over another's advantages, possessions etc., desire for something that another has) not Charity (Love) vaunteth (with much pride, boast) not in itself, is not puffed (giving undue praise) up.

What love will do!

Love bears pain just as Jesus Christ did on the cross for a people he had never seen or even established a relationship with. Love endures with long measurement just as Jesus endured the time hanging on the cross for you and I. Love is not temperamental. It doesn't start out strong and after a few hours stop loving even under extreme pressure. Love doesn't envy another person's blessings, possessions, advancements, or wishes to have the things of another person in envy. Love doesn't boast in them. Nor does love give it self-undue honor.

The Characteristics of Love

Let us take a closer look at what God's word tells us about love. How should it feel? What does it do? What does love not do? Let's get a better understanding about the Love that God birth in our hearts to have and maintain for eternity.

I Corinthians 13:5

"Doth not behave itself unseemly, seeketh not her own, is not easily provoked, thinketh no evil;"

- Does not behave itself unseemly (not decent or proper)
- Seeketh not her own (Love isn't selfish-searching to satisfy only one's self)
- Is not easily provoked (to excite to some action or feeling, to anger or irritate, not easily stirred up)

- Thinketh not evil (morally bad or wrong; wicked, harmful, injurious, unlucky, disastrous, wickedness; sin anything that causes harm; pain etc.)

Note: Love does not think of doing evil or concerning evil about another.

The Characteristics of Love

I Corinthians 13:6

"Rejoiceth not in iniquity, but rejoiceth in the truth;"

Rejoice not in iniquity (wickedness), but rejoices in truth (being true specific) sincerity; honesty conformity with fact, reality; actual existence correctness, accuracy, that which is true an established

Love does not rejoice in wickedness or evil. Love rejoices in truth! Love embraces truth and honesty. Love is attracted to reality and being correct. Love does not cling to untruth or dishonesty. Lies and dishonesty cannot abide where "TRUE" love is. True love reveals even the ugliest things in order to uphold honesty and trust in every relationship.

The Characteristics of Love

I Corinthians 13:7

"Beareth all things, believeth all things, hopeth all things, endureth all things"

Let's break down this scripture to get an even better understanding of what love does do.

- **Beareth all things**

Bearing: way of carrying and conducting oneself, a supporting part, endurance, the ability to last, stand pain)

- **All**: *entirely*
- **Things**: *multiple, any matter; affair or concern a happening, act, incident, event (a tangible object)*
- **Believeth all things**

Believe: to take as true, real—to trust a statement of promise of

- **All**: **entirely**
- **Things**: *multiple, any matter; affair or concern a happening, act, incident, event*
- **Hopeth all things**

Hope-a feeling that what is wanted will happen; desire accompanied by expectation
Entirely any matter

- **Edureth all things**

Endure: the ability to last, stand pain
All & Things: Entirely any matter, affair or concern a happening, act, incident, event

Love Bears, love believes, love hopes, love endures

The Characteristics of Love continued.....

Love believes beyond circumstances and situations. Love endures. Love has the ability to with stand pain, and suffering. Love stays in difficulty.

<u>I Corinthians 13:8</u>

"Charity never faileth; but whether there be prophecies, they shall fail; whether there be tongues, they shall cease; whether there be knowledge, it shall vanish away"

Charity never; not at any time and in no case faileth. Love at no point ever fails. Love never falls short and it is never weak. It never dies. It never stops operating in Love. Love is never negligent (habitually failing to do the required thing, neglectful; careless), but the word of God tells us that prophecies shall fail, tongues will cease (stop) and even knowledge will fade away.

The Characteristics of Love continued.....

How powerful is love that it will never ever fail? Why does it withstand beyond all things? The answer is because Love is God. God can't fail. God can not fade away. God is forever powerful this day and for eternity! Think about how we willingly give up the power that God has strengthened us with through and by love when we allow Love to escape from our hearts because of past hurts and disappointments. We have allowed the enemy to trick us in our families, in our marriages, with our children, in our churches and in our relationships concerning the matters of Love, and it's time we take back the power of Love that God has given us. It is time we stand together and be reunited in love.

Activity II

Activity II Part I

Now after getting a better understanding of what God describes Love as, let us take a look at some words that express Love the way that God describes it. Also, some words below will be a representative of the fruit begotten from possessing "real" Love.

Unselfish | patient | truth | suffers | long | kind | Envies no one | bears | believes | hopes | endures | Never fails | sympathetic | benevolent | measureable | Honesty | not easily irritated | acts appropriately |

<u>Activity II Part I continued....</u>

supportive | Real | true | tangible | Good | Great

| Happy | Smile | Support | Healing | Growth

Activity II

Activity II Part II

Let's have a brief discussion about the words in Activity II, Part II.

- Where do these words come from?
- How do these words make you feel?
- What are the differences between the words in Activity 1 compared to Activity II?
- In what types of places did you hear these words? For example, home, church, etc?
- How do you react when you hear these words?
- Is it easy for you to communicate with others using these words above?
- What are the benefits of using positive words versus using negative words?

Write your thoughts below for personal reflections:

_____

_____

_____

_____

_____

_____

_____

_____

_____

_____

_____

_____

_____

_____

_____

_____

_____

_____

A Brand New Love

After coming in contact with God's true definition of Love, do you feel different about how you felt about the word "Love?" Does God's true definition tangle itself with the mysteries and myths of what your mind and "heart" perceived love to be when you began your journey at the beginning of this book? Allow this very moment for the words that you have just read to soak into your heart and mind. Let these words penetrate your soul. Embrace what real love feels like. Take a deep breath, close your eyes and allow God to love up on you for a minute. Release the thoughts that were not from Him concerning love out of your mind, heart, and soul. Let Him heal and transform your mind so that you may receive the precious love that He has just for you.

****Love****

The Source of Love

We can continue in our studies in the Bible about love. The first book of John in the fourth chapter tells us what the source of Love is. This as we have discovered is God.

The bible tells us in **I John 4:7-21** where love comes from.

I John 4: 7-21

7: "Beloved, let us love one another; for Love is of God; and every one that loveth is born of God, and knoweth God.

8: He that loveth not, knoweth not God; for God is Love.

9: In this was manifested the love of God toward us, because that God sent his only begotten Son into the world, that we might live through him.

10: Here in is love, not that we loved God, but that he loved us, and sent his son to be the propitiation (to win the good will of) for our sins.

11: Beloved, if God so loved us, we ought also to love one another

12: No man hath seen God at any time, if we love one another, God dwelleth in us, and his love is perfected in us.

13: Hereby know we that we dwell in him, and he in us, because he hath given us of his Spirit."

The Source of Love

I John 4: 7-21 continued......

14: "And we have seen and do testify that the Father sent the Son to be the Savior of the world.

15: Whosoever shall confess that Jesus is the Son of God, God dwelleth in him, and he in God.

16: And we have known and believed the love that God hath to us. God is love; and he that dwelleth in love dwelleth in God, and God in him.

17: Herein is our love [2] made perfect, that we may have boldness in the Day of Judgment: because as he is, so are we in this world.

18: There is no fear in love; but perfect love casteth out fear: because fear hath torment. He that feareth is not made perfect in love.

19: We love him, because he first loved us.

20: If a man say, I love God, and hateth his brother, he is a liar: for he that loveth not his brother whom he hath seen, how can he love God whom he hath not seen?

21: And this commandment have we from him, That he who loveth God love his brother also."

GOD IS LOVE

Activity III

Activity III: Part I

Activity: Once you become more acquainted with God and His love for you, you will begin to feel things you never ever felt before. These emotions are transferred from His heart into yours. The words below reflect a few emotions that you will begin to feel in His amazing love.

Real | true | tangible | Good | Great | Happy | Smile

| Supported | Healing | Growth | Accomplishment

| Dedication | Positive | Laughter | Happiness |

Joy | Love | Passion | Energy | Amazing | Awesome

| Victorious | Healed | Complete | Successful |

<u>Activity III: Part I continued....</u>

Together | Unity | Strength | Motivated | Peace |

Stable | Endurance | Conqueror | I can Make It!

Activity III

Activity III: Part II

Let's have a brief discussion about any other emotions that may have surfaced regarding how the love of God makes "you" feel.

- Where do these words come from?
- How do these words make you feel?
- How is the love of God different from the world's concept of Love?
- What can you do to increase the amount of God's love in your life?
- What changes can you make to embrace the love of God more?

Write your thoughts below for personal reflections:

_____

_____

_____

_____

_____

_____

_____

_____

_____

_____

_____

_____

_____

_____

_____

God's Love

God's Love

God loves us so much that He gave His only begotten son for us. No greater love is there in all the Earth. How exciting is it to know how important and special you are to God! Once you tap into the Love of God and the Love our Personal Savior Jesus Christ has for you, your life will never ever be the same. You will begin to realize your worth. You are a treasure upon the earth... A child of the Most High God. A King's son or daughter... You are a prince or a princess. You are the Best there ever was. Your importance is immeasurable. You were made in and with perfection. Think on these things. For His thoughts towards you are not of evil but of good things. How awesome is it to know just how wonderful and great you are in His excellence and even more, how much He loves you?

As the word instructs us in the book of **John 15: 9 "As the Father hath loved me, so have I loved you:**

continue ye in my love." The ultimate goal of God's people is to see the glory of God upon the Earth in us through the Holy Spirit. Through the strength of Jesus Christ as the word also tells us in:

John 17: 24
"Father, I will that they also, whom thou hast given me, be with me where I am; that they may behold my glory, which thou hast given me: for thou lovedst me before the foundation of the world."

Love

We have come to the end of our journey. We have discovered so many new things together about love. Now, we know what happened in our history that displaced love in our families, in our communities, and churches. We know what Love is and most importantly who Love is. Love is God. After gaining so much insight on what Love is, we have become an empowered people and have the strength to move forward together as one body of Christ. We can begin to re-ignite Love back into our communities, our relationships and our churches and initiate the healing, the deliverance, the hope that we need to prepare and maintain us until the coming of our Lord. We are all now ambassadors for the kingdom of God. He has taught us directly from Heaven His divine revelation about love. You can now produce, replicate, and regenerate the growth of love in everyone with a willing heart that surrounds you.

Stimulate a heart today to love. Together we can spread the Love of God all over the world!

As you continue on with your own personal journey of Love with God, continue to pray and ask God for guidance to keep your heart saturated with His pure Love.

Thank you for coming along with me on this amazing journey my brothers and sisters in Christ. My prayer for you is that God's blessings; both spiritual and physical over take you, for His mercy to keep you, for His blood to protect you, and His peace remain with you always.